T0322191

Simon Gilham has built a multi-million strong community online for his commitment to saying the things that most people are too afraid to share or admit. This book is a curation of Simon's most impactful words and advice, so that you can be empowered to make the change you need, today.

Stop Lying to Yourself

Stop Lying to Yourself

101 Hard Truths to Help You Change Your Life

SIMON GILHAM

EBURY
PRESS

Ebury Press, an imprint of Ebury Publishing
20 Vauxhall Bridge Road
London SW1V 2SA

Ebury Press is part of the Penguin Random House group of companies
whose addresses can be found at global.penguinrandomhouse.com

Copyright © Simon Gilham 2024
Illustrations © Studio Noel

Simon Gilham has asserted his right to be identified as the author of this
Work in accordance with the Copyright, Designs and Patents Act 1988

First published by Ebury Press in 2024

www.penguin.co.uk

A CIP catalogue record for this book is available from the British Library

ISBN 9781529939194

Printed and bound in Great Britain by Clays Ltd, Elcograf S.p.A.

The authorised representative in the EEA is Penguin Random House
Ireland, Morrison Chambers, 32 Nassau Street, Dublin D02 YH68.

Penguin Random House is committed to a sustainable future for
our business, our readers and our planet. This book is made
from Forest Stewardship Council® certified paper.

*Dedicated to everyone who wonders
if I'm writing about them.*

I am.

INTRODUCTION

Firstly, I'd like to say thank you for picking up this book. *Stop Lying to Yourself* might seem like a harsh title, but I suspect that if you're reading this now, you're someone who realises they want to make a change in their life but are struggling to find the motivation and commitment to either start the process or follow through. Becoming the truest version of yourself can be hard work, but you should already feel proud of the stage you're at, having picked up this book.

This book, with its quotes and hard truths, should be seen as your most authentic best friend that will always keep it real with only your best interests at heart. It will be a tool for honest reflection, helping you to understand past mistakes that are not aligned with your vision of the happy and authentic life you wish to create for yourself, and therefore allowing you to break the cycle and leave the excuses behind. It will be a tool for motivation and a provider of strength, helping you overcome those mental obstacles that make giving up seem like an easy, acceptable way out.

This book had its early beginnings at the start of the Coronavirus pandemic. I was suddenly presented with a very different reality of my life, a life that I had never envisaged and had fought tirelessly to avoid. The early days were a real struggle to understand and cope with what was materialising. Being forced to live a new dictated life within an unknown timeline left me feeling confused, sad and, above all else, helpless.

As the weeks went on, I could see the impact the isolation and fear were having not only on myself but also on my children, family, friends and work colleagues. I could see mental health was becoming a prominently discussed symptom of the pandemic – something that had always previously been a little taboo. I started to reflect on my own feelings and search deep for happier memories to help keep me focused and strong. This journey of rediscovery took me to looking at old photos, listening to my favourite songs, and watching my favourite movies. In this book, I'm sharing my personal journey through some of the quotes that helped me. Most of these hard truths are my own, while a few are quotes I came across during that time. I don't know where they all came from, but I hope they can be as much help to you as they were to me, and that knowing I have gone through this process myself inspires and resonates, providing some level of strength to continue your own personal journey. The work I'm continuing with this book has allowed me to further develop the practical application of these quotes in a relatable way, helping to provide a framework for further insight.

Helping people create perspective in life and providing a sense of not being alone through connection, community, and sharing of experiences and emotions offers an opportunity to find collective strength through the realisation that you're not the only one experiencing these emotions or situations.

You'll never be too much for somebody who simply can't get enough of you.

The book has no specific order – it's a collective work of emotions that we all experience knowingly and unknowingly. Read the book from cover to cover, or pick up and put down the book as you wish … Start it in the middle and finish it at the start … My hope is that if this book can help to make your life just that little bit better, even for a moment, then that makes my work worthwhile.

I would like to express my heartfelt gratitude to all those who have supported me on this journey and continue to be a part of this amazing community.

As you read, I'd love to hear from you. Please post pictures of your favourite images, pages, quotes and experiences related to this book on social media using #SimonGilhamBook so I can like them and feature them on my page.

Love,

xGilham

101
HARD
TRUTHS

1

Life has a way of presenting you with the same lessons, disguised as different people until you grasp the message.

We all experience this. Each encounter with these lessons makes it clear that you can't escape your problems; they'll reappear in different forms until you learn from them and make a change. For example, if you don't learn from heartbreak, you'll likely experience it again, perhaps with a different person each time.

Through cultivating self-awareness and seeking deeper understanding, we can break cycles of repetition and embrace growth. Forgiveness, patience and a celebration of progress are essential in this journey. Remember, life's lessons are not meant to discourage, but to empower. Embrace them with courage, curiosity and a willingness to evolve – you'll pave the way for a more fulfilling existence.

2

If you don't know
if someone is the
right person to have
in your life, the next
time you're with
them ask yourself
this question: do
you love who you
are when you're
with them?

To determine if someone is right for you, reflect on how you feel about yourself when you're with them. Do you feel happy, respected and true to yourself? Or do you feel uneasy, insecure or unlike your real self? The right people in your life will make you feel comfortable and confident in who you are. They will bring out your best qualities and support you. Remember, healthy relationships should *enhance* your life, not diminish your sense of self-worth.

3

You give your life
meaning based
on the choices you
make. If you feel
life is meaningless,
the only person to
blame is yourself.

Your life's meaning is shaped by the choices *you* make. If you ever feel like life is meaningless, use it as a chance to think about your choices and mindset. It's not about blaming yourself, but instead taking charge of your journey. Every choice you make can bring depth, purpose and joy to your life. It's an invitation to reconsider your decisions, explore fulfilling paths and actively shape a life that feels meaningful to you.

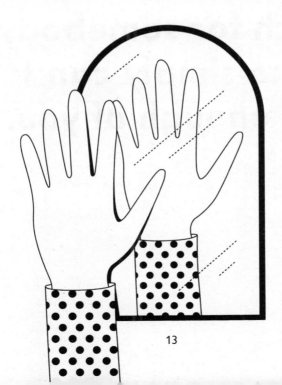

4

You'll never be too much for somebody who simply can't get enough of you.

If you ever feel like you're hard to love, remember, you're not the problem; you might just be asking the wrong person. The right person will appreciate every aspect of you and won't make you feel like you're too much or overwhelming. They'll be eager to understand and cherish all aspects of you. Embrace your unique qualities, and remember your worth is immeasurable to those who genuinely care about you and love you for who you are.

5

When you're quiet, you're heard only by those who genuinely care about you.

Often people are deaf to other people's pain, but the people who truly care about you will pay attention to the little things. They will notice the way your eyes light up when you're happy, or how your shoulders slump when you're feeling down. Words aren't needed. The magic of someone who truly cares about you is about being understood without saying a word.

6

There is no such thing as a perfect partner. Concentrate on finding someone who has many of the qualities you like and has similar values, and work on building a fantastic relationship.

7

Never fall in love
with the same
person twice,
because the second
time, you fall in love
with the memories,
not the person.

8

You came into their life to show them the meaning of true love, but they came into your life to show you the meaning of self-love.

Sometimes people come into our lives to teach us valuable lessons that we might not otherwise have learned. So, although it may seem exhausting, these types of people have helped you discover the power of self-love, and self-love is a journey that takes time (and a lot of effort!). It's about learning to value yourself, respecting your needs and taking care of yourself. Only when we truly love ourselves are we able to create a foundation for healthy future relationships with others. If someone has helped you to see the importance of self-love, be grateful that they entered your life, as they have helped you to establish higher standards for relationships, so you're less likely now to accept those who are not fulfilling your needs.

9

Some of us never found time to be happy because we were too busy trying to be strong.

When you're just pretending to be okay, behind that smile you hide a thousand tears and a world full of hurt. Trust me, it will eventually become too much and you'll be exhausted. You have to stop providing for others right now. Focus on you and start your mission to happiness and peace today!

10

The most confusing place a person can be is when you know there's a connection with someone, but you aren't officially together.

But you're not just friends either.

Being in a situation where there's a clear connection with someone but no official relationship can be incredibly confusing. It's a grey area between friendship and a committed relationship, filled with mixed signals and uncertainty. This in-between state can be emotionally challenging, as you're unsure of where you stand or what to expect. Communication is key in such situations. Discussing your feelings and desires openly can bring clarity, and either pave the way for a deeper relationship or help you understand if it's best to remain friends. Remember, clarity in your connections is crucial for emotional well-being.

(11)

Life is made up of games: select the game you wish to play, learn the rules and work out how to succeed.

Life will offer you various games you can choose to play. It's important to select areas that resonate with you, whether it's your career, relationships or personal interests. What matters most to you at the moment? Once you've chosen, invest time in understanding the 'rules' – the dynamics and skills you need to thrive in these areas. Success comes from strategically navigating these games, learning and adapting as you go. Remember, the key is not just choosing wisely but also committing to play your best in the game you've selected.

12

Someone who overthinks, over-loves.

Being someone who 'overthinks and over-loves' signifies a deep and passionate approach to relationships. It means you invest a lot of thought and emotion into the people you care about. While this depth of feeling can lead to profound connections and meaningful experiences, it can also bring moments of vulnerability and anxiety. It's important to find balance between thoughtful consideration and letting go of unnecessary worry. Embracing self-compassion, open communication with loved ones and setting healthy boundaries can help manage the intensity of your love and thoughts. Remember that your capacity to love deeply is a beautiful quality, and with self-awareness and self-compassion, it can enhance your relationships in meaningful ways.

13

Today is not easy, tomorrow is more difficult.

But the day after tomorrow will be wonderful.

Cultivate resilience and optimism. In challenging moments, remember that tough times are temporary. Focus on developing strategies to navigate the difficulties ahead, knowing that they pave the way for a brighter future. Work on cultivating patience, resilience and a positive mindset. By facing today's challenges head-on, you're not only preparing for tomorrow but setting the foundation for the wonderful days that lie ahead. Keep moving forward with optimism and determination.

What is a best friend?

It's someone who can see the truth and pain in you, even when you're fooling everyone else.

A best friend is a unique individual who possesses the keen insight to recognise and understand your genuine emotions and struggles, even when you're adeptly masking them from the rest of the world. This definition underscores the deep connection and intuitive understanding that characterises such a friendship. It highlights the idea that a best friend is not just someone who shares your joys and successes, but someone who can discern and empathise with your hidden pains and truths, offering support and companionship during times when you might feel most alone.

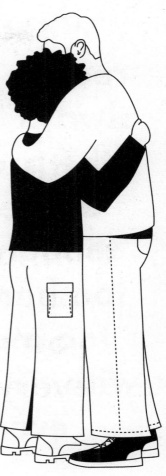

15

What you don't realise is that she's always felt like she's the problem. Her entire life, she's thought that she's too hard to love or too much to deal with. That's all she's ever known!

Realise that if she constantly feels like she's the problem, it's often due to long-standing self-doubt and feeling unworthy of love. It's important to offer consistent support and reassurance. Help her see her own value and that she's deserving of love and happiness. Encourage open communication and understanding. Show her that she's appreciated and loved just as she is. Building someone's self-esteem is a gradual process, but with patience and care, she can learn to see herself in a more positive light.

(16)

Stop checking your phone over and over again.

Yeah, they're active online ... but not for you!

Yeah, they're free ... but not for you.

While you're waiting for a text from them, they're waiting for a text from someone else.

Try to ease the urge to check your phone repeatedly. If someone's not reaching out or making time for you, recognise it. Redirect your attention to those who value and prioritise your presence. It's empowering to step back and assess relationships, making room for connections that reciprocate your effort and interest. Prioritise your own well-being and invest time in those who genuinely appreciate and care about you.

17

You will never be able to heal by going back to what broke you.

Often, there's a temptation to revisit past relationships or situations in hopes of finding closure or rekindling what was lost; however, this can hinder the healing process. Healing begins with the understanding that going back to what caused your pain rarely leads to recovery. Instead, focus on building a future where you are no longer defined by past hurts. This involves acknowledging the pain, learning from the experience and then letting go. Instead, surround yourself with people and activities that support your growth and happiness – what does this look like for you? Remember, healing's a journey that requires stepping away from the past and embracing the possibilities of a new beginning.

18

Real relationships, the ones that last, require a lot of forgiveness. You have to accept that your partner isn't perfect and will hurt you, disappoint you and upset you. You have to figure out if you're willing to go through the ups and downs with them.

You might be a perfect match when you first meet, but as you grow older, you evolve into different people. Over the years your wants and needs change. As humans, we grow and transform. It's also important to accept that your partner is not perfect. They may hurt you, disappoint you and upset you at times. The key is deciding whether you're willing to intentionally evolve and navigate the ups and downs together, because that's what love is truly about.

Control your emotions: learn to react less and instead respond.

Gain control over your emotions and practise reacting less impulsively. Emotions can cloud our judgement and lead to hasty responses. Take a moment to pause, breathe and think before reacting. This allows you to respond more thoughtfully and make better decisions. Learning to manage your emotions can lead to improved relationships and a more balanced life. Embrace emotional intelligence to navigate challenges with composure and wisdom.

20

This is a little harsh, but ... they were supposed to hurt you.

And you were supposed to sit in your pain for a while.

This isn't because you deserve it; it's not a form of punishment. It's because it was the only way that you could shake off that old version of you, the version that actually thought the bare minimum could ever be considered effort.

You needed this pain to wake you up, because otherwise you would never grow and become the person you're supposed to be. Remember, growth often starts with discomfort. You're worth it!

21

Keep the good ones close to your heart and let them know you appreciate them.

Treasure the good people in your life. Recognise and appreciate those who bring positivity, love and support. These cherished connections enrich your life and bring happiness. Prioritise these relationships, nurture them and let them be a source of joy. By keeping the good ones close, you create a circle of love and support that enhances your well-being.

22

Some people talk to you in their free time and some people free their time to talk to you. Make sure you know the difference between the two.

23

I'm not expecting an apology. I just hope one day you feel sorry for the way you treated me.

If a man truly wants you, you won't have to ask for effort. He'll call you, he'll text you, he'll make time. No man is too busy for a woman he truly wants.

It's important to value yourself and recognise the level of effort someone is willing to give in a relationship. When a person genuinely wants to be with you, they will naturally prioritise you and will make efforts to show their interest and commitment. They'll communicate, make plans and integrate you into their life without you feeling the need to prompt or question their intentions. You need to understand your worth and never settle for minimal effort or inconsistent attention. Set standards for how you want to be treated and recognise that a partner who truly values you will make you a clear priority in their life. It's about not just hearing promises, but seeing actions that align with those words and fostering a healthy, reciprocal and respectful relationship.

25

Your happiness is largely your responsibility.

While external factors can influence your mood, *you* have the power to choose how you react and the actions you take. Prioritise self-care, positive thinking and personal growth. Take charge of your own well-being by focusing on what brings you joy and fulfilment. By recognising your role in your happiness, you can navigate life's ups and downs with resilience and create a more content and satisfying life. What's the first step you're going to take (no matter how small) to take responsibility for your happiness?

What is one thing you are holding on to that you know you need to let go of?

Identify something in your life that's holding you back, be it a grudge, a fear or an unhealthy habit. Acknowledge its impact on you. Understand that letting go is a step towards personal growth.

Start small; gradually detach yourself from this burden. Replace it with positive thoughts or actions. Remember, releasing what no longer serves you creates space for new, healthier experiences. Embrace this change for a happier, more fulfilling life.

27

Being called 'sensitive' for reacting to disrespect is manipulation at its finest.

Labelling someone as 'sensitive' for reacting to disrespect is a manipulative tactic. It invalidates legitimate feelings and shifts the blame, suggesting the problem is the person's reaction rather than the disrespectful behaviour. This is a form of gaslighting, where the intention is to make you doubt your own feelings and responses. Trust your instincts and emotions. It's perfectly valid to feel upset when disrespected, and standing up for yourself is a sign of self-respect and emotional intelligence, not over-sensitivity.

28

The journey to self-acceptance begins with letting go of who you think you should be.

Starting to truly accept yourself begins when you let go of who you think you need to be. It's about peeling off the layers of expectations and what everyone else says you should be like. It's a gentle journey where you learn to appreciate the real you, flaws and all. This doesn't happen overnight. It's a process whereby you learn to see your quirks and differences as strengths. By being kind to yourself and understanding that change takes time, you start living more authentically. Remember, every step towards being your true self is a step towards deep self-acceptance.

If someone can fall asleep knowing you're crying, knowing you're hurting and your heart is broken, then they don't love you in the way you deserve.

If you find yourself in a situation where your emotional pain is disregarded by someone you care about, it's a significant indicator of their feelings and respect towards you. Recognise that genuine love involves empathy, concern and a deep desire to alleviate the pain of loved ones. You need to acknowledge the situation's reality and prioritise your emotional health. Reflect on the relationship and consider if it's truly reciprocal and caring. Instead, surround yourself with people who genuinely value and support you. Don't be afraid to seek help or talk to someone trustworthy about your feelings. Your emotional well-being is paramount, and it's okay to distance yourself from those who consistently negate or ignore your feelings.

30

When you are honest, you lose people who don't deserve you.

Being truthful is essential for your integrity and self-respect. Those who can't handle your honesty are not worth keeping in your life. Surround yourself with people who appreciate your authenticity and respect your values. In the long run, honesty attracts genuine connections and builds stronger relationships with those who truly deserve your presence.

31

Don't like me?
Fuck off.
Problem solved.

It's okay if not everyone likes you; what's most important is how you feel about yourself and making sure you invest your energy in relationships and activities that bring you joy and fulfilment. Take care of yourself by establishing limits and concentrating on your personal growth and happiness. Remember, your self-worth isn't determined by others' opinions. By letting go of the need for universal acceptance, you free yourself to live authentically and contentedly.

Sometimes
the reason why
good things aren't
happening to you
is because you
are the very good
thing that needs to
happen to other
people.

Sometimes, when good things don't happen to you right away, it's because you have a special purpose. You might be a kind and compassionate person who makes others feel better, or the one who helps people through tough times. Your good deeds and kindness are making a difference in the world, even if you don't realise it. So, keep being yourself, and know that you're making a difference.

33

Small circle, private life, peaceful mind, happy heart.

Keep a small circle for a private life, and you'll find a peaceful mind and a happy heart. Quality matters more than quantity when it comes to relationships. Embrace simplicity and prioritise those who bring positivity and support to your life. Protect your peace by surrounding yourself with genuine and trustworthy individuals. A smaller, close-knit circle can lead to a more fulfilling and contented life. Choose your inner circle wisely and focus on the joy it brings.

**If you can
love the wrong
person that much,
imagine how much
you could truly love
the right person.**

Loving the wrong person takes a huge amount of effort, but the end result is always going to be incomplete. Loving the right person with the same amount of effort will be much more rewarding and long-lasting. Don't waste your efforts.

35

No matter how hard you try, you cannot force someone to be with you.

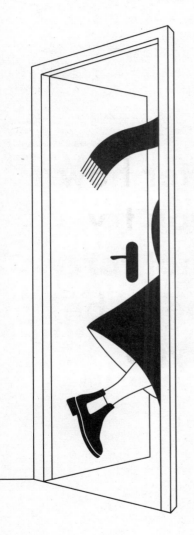

Don't compel anyone to stay in your life; if they decide to leave, that's their loss. Sometimes, people don't understand how amazing you are until they meet others who aren't anything like you.

You know it's over
when you're more
in love with the
memories than with
the person standing
right in front of you.

It's a clear indication that it's time to move on when your attachment to the way things used to be outweighs your focus on the present. If you find yourself reminiscing about the past more than embracing the present, it's a sign that things aren't working. It's okay to let go. Seek someone who brings happiness to your present moments.

37

A best friend isn't one who makes your problems disappear; a best friend is one who doesn't disappear when you're facing your problems.

A true best friend isn't someone who makes your problems vanish, but someone who stands by your side when you're dealing with them. Genuine friendship is about support, loyalty and being there through thick and thin. Value those who stay with you during your toughest moments, as they are the ones who truly care about your well-being. Who are these people in your life? Remember, in times of trouble, the presence and support of a best friend can make all the difference, offering strength and comfort when you need it most.

If a man hurts every woman who enters his life, it's because his true soulmate is a man.

Himself.

When a man repeatedly hurts others in relationships, it often indicates he's indirectly harming himself. This pattern can be a manifestation of deep-seated personal struggles or unresolved issues. Such behaviours not only damage his relationships but also his own emotional well-being. It's crucial for him to recognise this self-destructive cycle and seek ways to understand and heal his own internal conflicts. Healing oneself is the first step towards building healthier and more respectful relationships with others.

39

If you self-isolate when you get upset, it might be because you were left to deal with your emotions alone as a child.

If you tend to want to be alone when you're upset, it might be because, as a child, you had to handle your feelings by yourself. Knowing this can help you understand why you self-isolate. Be kind to yourself and try sharing your feelings with friends or family you trust. It's okay to ask for support. Create healthy ways to deal with emotions, like writing in a journal or talking to someone who understands you. By doing this, you can break the habit of isolating yourself and build stronger connections with others, making it easier to handle tough times together.

40

You didn't become selfish, you became harder to manipulate.

Don't confuse the two.

Sometimes, when you start saying no to people who are trying to push you around, they might call you selfish. But really, you're just getting better at not letting others take advantage of you. It's like learning to stand up for yourself and not letting someone else control your choices. Remember, it's okay to think about what's best for you and not just do what others want all the time. That's not being selfish, that's being smart and strong!

41

One day you're going to meet someone who makes you realise that there was never anything wrong with you.

Meeting someone who truly appreciates you can be a powerful experience. It can make you realise that any doubts or criticisms you faced before weren't about you, but were reflections of the wrong relationships or situations. This person will help you see your true worth and uniqueness. You've *always* been enough, but it sometimes takes the right person to help you see and believe it. Such relationships are a reminder of the importance of being valued and understood for who you are.

42

You can't cheat
on someone you're
in love with. It's not
possible, because
if you truly loved
them, cheating
would never be
an option.

True love is more than just butterflies; it's the quiet comfort of finding your home in another. It's a daily choice, valuing them not for ease, but because they're your greatest treasure. When doubts arise, remember the laughter you share, and the dreams you've built together. Consider whether fleeting thrills are worth risking what you've built. Opt for trust, honesty and a love that resonates deeply. Cherish your bond, and together, build a love stronger than any temptation. If temptation still lingers or thoughts of betrayal surface, it's a sign to re-evaluate your relationship or personal values. Cultivate open communication, confront issues head-on or, if necessary, consider moving on with integrity and respect. Remember, true love should build, not fracture, trust.

43

One of the most fucked up things the universe will do to you is let you meet the right person at the wrong time.

Life has a way of presenting complex situations,
like introducing you to the right person at what seems
like the wrong time. It can feel incredibly frustrating
and unfair. This experience teaches us about the
unpredictable nature of life and relationships. It's
a reminder that timing plays a crucial role in how
relationships
unfold. Sometimes,
all you can do
is accept the
situation, learn
from it and keep
moving forward,
hoping that if it's
meant to be, the
universe will align
things in your
favour when the
time is right.

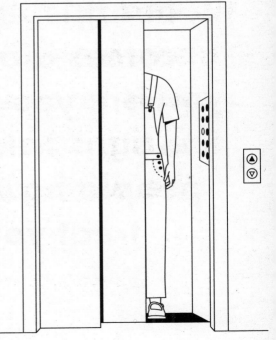

44

Regardless of how good your heart is, there comes a point where you have to start treating people how they treat you.

While kindness is valuable, it's equally important to recognise when you should acknowledge the treatment you receive. If someone consistently disrespects or mistreats you, it's okay to adjust your behaviour towards them accordingly. This isn't about retaliation, but about protecting your well-being and ensuring mutual respect in your interactions. Remember, maintaining your own dignity is as important as being good-hearted.

(45) **If you weren't invited, don't go. If none of your friends told you, don't ask. If you got a late invite, respectfully decline. They had no intention of including you in the first place.**

Respect yourself enough to recognise when you're not genuinely wanted in a situation. If you're not invited initially, don't impose yourself. If you're not informed about an event by friends, don't push for inclusion. A late invite can often be an afterthought; consider declining it with dignity. Value your worth and spend time with people who truly appreciate and include you from the start. Your self-respect and the company of sincere friends are far more important than fitting in where you're not valued.

46

Don't put me in a position where I've got to show you how heartless I can be. You might never look at me the same.

You must establish your boundaries firmly. Warn others against pushing you to a point where your less forgiving side surfaces, a change that could irreversibly alter their perception of you. Everyone has their limits, and respecting those limits is crucial for healthy relationships. Stand your ground with clarity and strength, ensuring others understand the seriousness of overstepping your boundaries. This isn't just about self-preservation; it's about maintaining mutual respect and understanding in all interactions.

47

Stay away from people who have benefitted from you but act like you have never given them anything.

Value yourself by avoiding people who disregard your generosity. If someone consistently takes advantage of your help without acknowledgement or gratitude, it's a sign to reassess that relationship. You deserve to be around those who appreciate and reciprocate your kindness. Protect your energy and invest in relationships that are balanced and respectful. Remember, your efforts and contributions are significant, and you should be treated with appreciation, not indifference.

No woman leaves because her partner made a mistake. She left because he made it a habit. Just because she's always been there doesn't mean she'll always be there.

No woman typically leaves a relationship solely due to a single error; it is often the repetitive nature of mistakes that leads to a departure. This reflects the truth that many women prefer to work through challenges with their existing partner rather than beginning anew with someone else. Her continued presence in the relationship is indicative of her hope that you would rise to the occasion and become the partner she deserves. However, a false sense of security in her loyalty can lead to taking her for granted and disrespecting her. The crucial lesson here is never to assume that someone's unwavering support in the past guarantees their presence in the future. Continuous effort and respect are essential in maintaining a healthy, enduring relationship.

49

People don't understand the stress of trying to explain what's happening in your mind when you can't even comprehend it yourself.

When you're feeling
really mixed up inside
and can't explain why,
remember it's totally
okay. It's like having a
jumbled puzzle in your
head that you can't
solve right away. Be
kind to yourself and
remember that lots of
people feel this way
sometimes. Instead

of trying to figure it all out at once, do things that
make you feel calm and happy. This could be drawing,
listening to music or spending time outside. Writing
down your thoughts in a notebook can help too, like
a diary where you can say anything you want. And if
you're really stuck, it can help to talk to someone you
trust. People you can confide in are like guides who can
help you understand the puzzle in your head.

50

If you wake up every morning because of them, if they found you at your lowest and picked you up, if they make you smile more than you ever believed possible, if they gave you a reason to live again, just know you've found your forever person, so don't ever give up on them.

51

Fail forward: learn from every single mistake you make.

52

One of the most toxic traits a person can have is expecting you to be okay with something when they wouldn't be okay with it if the roles were switched.

Recognise and avoid double standards in relationships. If someone expects you to tolerate behaviour they wouldn't accept themselves, it's unfair. Aim for mutual respect and equality. Speak up against unequal expectations and strive for a balanced, healthy relationship. Remember, what's good for one should be acceptable for both.

53

Don't be sad that people talk about you behind your back: they're in the right place.

Behind you!

When you find out people are talking about you behind your back, consider it a sign that you're progressing in life. Use this as a chance to concentrate on your own journey and personal development, instead of getting involved in negativity. Remember, your actions and character speak louder than rumours or gossip. By staying true to yourself and moving forward, you naturally elevate yourself above those who focus on negativity.

54

The hardest goodbyes often lead to the most meaningful hellos.

Saying goodbye, especially to something or someone significant in our life, can be incredibly tough. These moments challenge us, pushing us out of our comfort zones and forcing us to confront change. However, it's in these difficult farewells that we pave the way for new beginnings. Each goodbye carries with it the promise of a new hello, an opportunity for growth and discovery. Embrace the uncertainty and let it guide you towards unexpected joys and opportunities. Remember, it's through the toughest goodbyes that we find the strength to welcome the most meaningful hellos, opening our hearts to new people, experiences and lessons that enrich our lives.

A man often leaves a woman for another woman.

But a woman leaves a man for herself.

Typically, when a man leaves a relationship, it's to pursue another woman, a choice driven by external desires. However, when a woman decides to leave, it's often an act of profound self-realisation. She isn't just leaving a man; she's choosing herself. This decision is a powerful statement of self-respect and independence. It's about recognising her own needs, worth and potential for happiness outside the confines of the relationship. Such departures are bold affirmations of self-love and personal empowerment, reflecting a deep commitment to one's own well-being and growth.

56

When I tell you
I love you, I don't
say it out of habit.
I say it to remind
you that you're the
best thing that's
ever happened
to me.

These words are chosen intentionally to convey the profound impact you may have on someone's life. By saying 'I love you', it emphasises that your presence in my life is deeply valued and appreciated and that you are considered one of my greatest blessings. This expression serves as an affirmation of my sincere feelings and of how special you really are, highlighting the joy and significance you bring. These are words we all want to hear at least once in our lifetime, and there is someone out there for all of us that makes these words a living reality. Each of us deserves a love that feels genuine, where 'I love you' is not just a phrase but a promise of unwavering support, understanding and lifelong companionship. As we journey through life, it's about recognising and embracing the love that aligns with our worth, making us feel cherished, understood and truly valued.

57

If you stress too much about something before it happens, you put yourself through it twice.

When you excessively worry about a future event, you essentially experience the stress and anxiety of that situation twice. The initial phase of stress occurs in anticipation, as you mentally and emotionally grapple with the potential outcomes and challenges. This preemptive worry often magnifies the actual event's impact, leading to a heightened sense of anxiety and concern. In this way you not only endure the stress in the moment but also suffer through it in advance, doubling the emotional toll. It's important to manage anticipatory anxiety and maintain a balanced perspective to avoid unnecessary pre-stress.

If a friendship lasts longer than seven years, psychologists say it will last a lifetime.

It is psychological observation that friendships that last beyond seven years are likely to be lifelong relationships. The seven-year mark is considered significant because it often means the friendship has withstood various challenges and transitions, such as changes in life circumstances, personal growth and evolving interests. Over time, these friendships develop a strong foundation of mutual understanding, shared history and emotional bonds. The longevity suggests a deep level of commitment and connection, indicating that such friendships have the resilience and depth to endure throughout the ups and downs of life.

(59)

No matter how good your heart is, you won't always get good things in return, and that sucks because there are so many good people out there, and they get hurt all the time.

Having a good heart doesn't always guarantee receiving good in return, which can be a harsh reality to accept. It's especially tough knowing that many kind-hearted people face hurt and disappointment. However, the value of your goodness isn't diminished by others' actions or life's unfair moments. It's important to continue being kind and true to your values, not for the sake of reward, but because it defines who you are. Embracing this is important for your inner peace and satisfaction, knowing you've chosen to spread positivity in a world that doesn't always reciprocate it.

Do you ever wish you had the chance to meet someone again for the first time, so you could just run like hell in the opposite direction?

Sometimes we encounter people who bring negativity into our lives. It's okay to wish you hadn't met them. Learn to recognise such relationships early on. Trust your instincts and don't be afraid to distance yourself from those who drain your energy or happiness. Prioritise your well-being and surround yourself with positive influences. Remember, it's never too late to create boundaries and choose a healthier path for yourself.

Feelings that return are ones that never truly departed.

Feelings that resurface often indicate unresolved emotions or connections. It's important to acknowledge these feelings and understand their root cause. Reflect on why these emotions are returning and what they mean to you. Sometimes they can signify unfinished business or a deep, lasting attachment. It's crucial to deal with these feelings honestly and thoughtfully, whether it leads to closure, healing or rekindling a relationship. Remember, it's normal for emotions to ebb and flow, but understanding them is key to your emotional well-being.

If you could choose anyone you've ever met to knock on your front door right now, who would it be?

Think about someone who brings joy, comfort or inspiration into your life. This could be a loved one, a friend or even someone you admire. Imagine them knocking on your door right now. How does that make you feel? Use this feeling as a guide to understand who positively impacts your life. Seek to spend more time with such people and strive to be that person for others too. Surrounding yourself with positive influences can greatly enhance your happiness and well-being.

63

Are you seriously chasing someone who doesn't want you? Have some self-respect and walk away!

You deserve better.

64

I know.

I know it's tough.

I know you're struggling.

But do me a favour: don't give up.

Better days are just around the corner, trust me.

The worst feeling is when you finally get over your depression, you fall in love, and you get your heart broken again.

Recovering from heartbreak can be incredibly tough. Remember, healing is not linear and setbacks happen. Focus on your well-being and surround yourself with supportive people. Allow yourself to feel and process your emotions, but also remember your strength and resilience. You've overcome challenges before and you can do it again. Keep building your self-worth and don't let this setback define you. Your ability to love and be loved remains intact, and better experiences await you.

66

Let me make this simple:

You ghost me,
I ghost you.

You show me no interest,
I'll show you no effort.

You put me second,
I'll put you last.

But if you show me loyalty and love, I'll give you the world.

Relationships thrive on reciprocity. If someone ghosts you or shows no interest, it's okay to protect your own feelings and do the same. Prioritise those who value you. When someone demonstrates loyalty and love, reciprocate with care and appreciation. Healthy connections are built on mutual effort and respect. Surround yourself with those who deserve your love and be open to giving your all to those who reciprocate your feelings.

You haven't met all the people who are going to love you yet, and you haven't met all the people you are going to love within your lifetime.

This offers a heartening reminder that life is a continuous journey of forming new relationships. It emphasises that there are still many individuals you have yet to encounter who will come to hold a special place in your heart through love and affection. Similarly, there are numerous people who will come to love and cherish you in the future. This perspective fosters hope and excitement for the future, underscoring the endless possibilities for meaningful connections and relationships that await you in the journey of life.

It encourages an optimistic outlook and reassures you that the realm of love and companionship is ever-expanding and evolving.

Some say it's painful to wait for someone, and some say it's painful to forget someone.

But the worst pain is when you don't know whether to wait or forget.

Being unsure whether to wait for someone or to move on can be hard. In such situations, listen to your intuition and consider your own well-being. If waiting causes more hurt and uncertainty, it might be healthier to let go. Focus on activities and relationships that bring you peace and joy – make a list of these for yourself now. Making a decision, whether to wait or forget, can bring clarity and relief from the pain of uncertainty.

You had many reasons to stay, but you chose to leave. I had many reasons to leave, but I chose to stay.

In relationships, we often face tough choices. Sometimes, a person who might have many reasons to stay will still feel compelled to leave, maybe due to personal needs or unresolved issues. On the flip side, you might find numerous reasons to leave but choose to stay, driven by commitment and hope for what the relationship could become. This complexity shows that decisions in love are deeply personal and not always based on clear-cut reasons.

70

They say love comes when you're not ready but ends when you are.

Love often arrives unexpectedly, showing us that we don't always need to be fully prepared for it. It teaches us flexibility and the beauty of surprise. Conversely, love might end when we feel most ready to embrace it, reminding us that we can't control everything. This unpredictability encourages us to live in the moment and appreciate love when it's present. Remember, readiness for love is less about perfect timing and more about being open to the lessons and experiences it brings. Trust the process. You need to go through the hard times to make you the person you are today: life is learning, not teaching.

The lesson you struggle with will repeat itself until you learn from it.

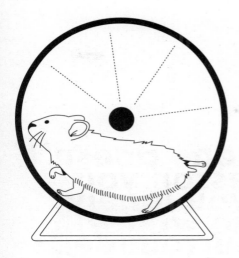

Life's lessons will keep reappearing until you grasp them. When you face the same challenges repeatedly, it's an opportunity to learn and grow. Reflect on the patterns and choices that lead to these lessons. Embrace self-awareness and take steps to change and evolve. By learning from these experiences, you break the cycle and move towards a more fulfilling life. Remember, personal growth comes from understanding and applying the lessons life presents to you.

72

Being alone doesn't make you lonely; being surrounded by the wrong people does.

Loneliness isn't about being alone; it's about being with the wrong people. Surround yourself with those who uplift and support you. Quality connections matter more than quantity. Choose relationships that bring positivity and fulfilment. If you're alone, use that time to build a strong relationship with yourself – what can you do by yourself that you might enjoy? A walk in the park, visiting a new café, cooking yourself a nourishing meal, starting a new hobby? It's better to be alone and content than in the company of those who make you feel lonely.

73

Not everyone is going to like you or wish the best for you in life, and you're never going to be able to make everyone happy no matter how hard you try.

You can't control what other people think: it's impossible to please everyone. Some people might hold on to grudges or harbour long-term resentment towards you, perhaps due to professional success or past conflicts within social circles. Remember that you can only control your own actions and words, not how others react to them. Focus on being the best version of yourself: be kind, be honest, be respectful and be true to who you are. Don't for a second deprive the world of your beautiful light because of the darkness of others.

74

Feeling sad after making a decision doesn't necessarily mean it was the wrong one.

Experiencing sadness after a decision doesn't always indicate it was wrong. Choices can bring mixed emotions, even when they're the best for your growth or well-being. Trust your judgement and understand that growth often involves stepping out of your comfort zone, which can be emotional. Embrace the process and learn from the experience. Remember, your feelings are valid, and they can coexist with the knowledge that you made the right decision for your long-term happiness and fulfilment.

When I used to hear your name, it would give me something that it doesn't give me anymore ... a smile.

You will never find the right person if you never let go of the wrong one.

There are two types of tired: one is when your body is screaming for sleep, and the other is when your body is screaming for peace.

Recognise the two types of tiredness. Physical tiredness signals the need for rest, while emotional tiredness indicates a need for inner peace. Pay attention to your body's messages. Rest when you're physically tired, but also seek inner peace when you're emotionally drained. Engage in activities that calm your mind and nourish your soul. Prioritise yourself to find a balance between physical and emotional well-being. Remember, taking care of both aspects is essential for overall health and happiness. It's about honouring what your body truly needs and creating a holistic approach to caring for yourself for a more rejuvenated and fulfilled life.

Can we please stop telling people, 'Yeah but that's your mum/dad/ brother/sister.' You have a right to walk away from people who constantly keep hurting you.

Family or not, toxicity is toxicity. Don't let a blood relationship excuse harmful behaviour. You have the right to distance yourself from anyone who consistently hurts you, especially in situations marked by selfishness and disloyalty. Prioritise your well-being and mental health by setting boundaries and surrounding yourself with those who uplift and support you. Recognise that in the face of selfish and disloyal actions, choosing to protect yourself is not selfish; it's a valid and essential choice. Your happiness and peace matter, regardless of who is involved. Don't be afraid to prioritise yourself, particularly when confronted with actions that jeopardise your well-being.

79

When are you going to finally realise that what's coming is better than what's gone?

Recognise that the future holds opportunities and experiences that can surpass what you've lost or left behind. Letting go of the past opens doors to new possibilities. Embrace change and look forward with optimism. Trust that life has more to offer and that each ending is a chance for a new beginning. Stay hopeful and open to the potential of what lies ahead, as it often brings growth and happiness you might not have imagined.

80

The road to self-discovery is often paved with discomfort and uncertainty.

Embarking on the journey of self-discovery is not a path of ease; it's a road marked by moments of discomfort and elements of uncertainty. These challenges, however, are not roadblocks but rather stepping stones leading us towards a deeper understanding of who we are. It is through confronting these uneasy feelings and embracing the unknown that we grow and evolve. This process invites us to question, to explore and to break free from the confines of our former selves. As we navigate this terrain, we learn to trust in our resilience and find solace in the fact that, with every step forward, we are shaping a more authentic version of ourselves.

81

Faking a smile is easier than explaining the pain you're in.

Faking a smile can sometimes feel simpler than explaining the pain inside. It's okay to protect your feelings when necessary, but don't hide your pain indefinitely. Seek support and share your emotions with trusted friends or professionals. Opening up can be a path to healing and understanding. Remember, it's important to address your pain and not carry it alone. There's strength in vulnerability, and seeking help can lead to better and brighter days ahead. You don't have to suffer in silence; there are people who care and are willing to listen.

82

If you have to choose between me and another person, choose the other person. Because if you truly cared about me, you wouldn't need to choose.

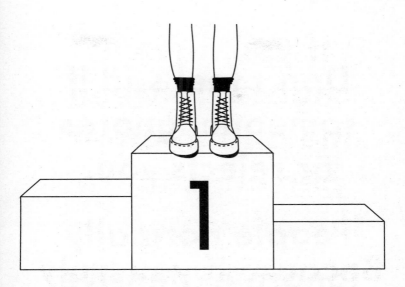

You should never be someone's option, find yourself living in fear of being a second choice, or feel replaceable. No matter how much it may hurt, make yourself a priority by walking away!

83

Don't feel sad if someone ignores or rejects you.

People normally ignore expensive things because they can't afford them.

Don't let someone's ignorance or rejection make you sad. People sometimes overlook valuable things because they can't appreciate their worth. Your value isn't determined by how others perceive you. Focus on your self-worth and the people who appreciate you for who you are. Keep your confidence high by surrounding yourself with those who see the treasure you are. Don't let others' ignorance affect your self-esteem; you are valuable just as you are.

One day, someone's going to walk into your life and make you realise why it never worked out with anyone else.

One day, someone special will enter your life, and you'll understand why previous relationships didn't work out. Trust that the right person is worth the wait. Until then, focus on self-improvement and self-love. Be open to new connections, but don't rush. This person will bring you the happiness and fulfilment you deserve. Patience is key. Sometimes the best things come when you least expect them. Remember, your future holds the possibility of a deep and meaningful connection that will make past heartaches worth it.

85

I have a question for you: if you only had five minutes left to live, who would be the one person that you would like to have your last conversation with?

Close your eyes and let your mind run away with this one. Consider who truly matters to you in your final moments. The person you'd want to have your last conversation with should be someone who holds a special place in your heart, someone you love and care about deeply. It could be a family member, a close friend or a partner. Use this reflection to prioritise meaningful relationships in your life. Cherish the time you have with loved ones and make an effort to express your feelings and create lasting memories. Remember, the people who bring joy and love into your life are the ones worth connecting with.

86

Have you ever gone to sleep only to wake up feeling tired?

Your mind never found peace; it wasn't truly rested.

Waking up tired often means your mind didn't find peace while you slept. Before bedtime, focus on calming activities like meditation, writing or journalling. Create a routine that tells your mind it's time to relax. By making your mental space peaceful, you'll improve sleep quality and wake up feeling refreshed. Remember, finding inner peace is key to true rest and overall well-being. Sleep becomes your refuge, a means to temporarily escape the world.

Perhaps it won't work out, but discovering if it does will be the greatest adventure ever.

Maybe it won't work out, but the journey to find out is an incredible adventure. Embrace the uncertainty of new experiences, for they hold the potential for amazing discoveries. Don't let fear of failure hold you back from exploring new paths and opportunities. Life's greatest adventures often come from taking risks and pursuing the unknown. Whether it succeeds or not, the journey itself is a valuable and enriching experience. So, dare to embark on the adventure of discovering what's possible, and relish the excitement of the unknown.

88

Learn to be happy in your own company.

Embrace solitude as an opportunity for self-discovery and contentment. When you find joy within yourself, you become less reliant on external factors for happiness. Self-contentment is a valuable skill that allows you to enjoy life independently. Cultivate self-love by pursuing your passions and savouring moments of solitude. What have you done by yourself today? How did you feel while you were doing it? By learning to be happy on your own, you can lead a more fulfilling and balanced life.

89

You're not stressed because you're doing too much; you're stressed because you're doing too little of what makes you feel most alive.

Stress often comes from neglecting what truly energises you, not from doing too much. Prioritise activities that ignite your passion and joy. When you engage in what makes you feel alive, you'll find balance and reduce stress. Don't just exist; live with purpose and do more of what nourishes your soul. Your well-being is worth the effort. Remember, a fulfilling life includes time for what brings you happiness and vitality.

90

The most profound relationships are not those without conflict, but those where conflicts lead to greater understanding.

In every relationship, conflicts are inevitable. But instead of fearing or avoiding them, embrace conflicts as opportunities for growth. When disagreements arise, approach them with an open heart and a willingness to listen. Seek to understand the other person's perspective and communicate your own honestly. By navigating conflicts together, you'll not only resolve issues but also strengthen your bond through mutual respect and deeper understanding. It's in the midst of conflict that the most profound relationships are forged.

(91)

You can be the whole package and still end up at the wrong address. When this happens, the receiver will mishandle you because:

1. They don't know what to do with you, and

2. They were never meant to have you in the first place.

Even if you're the whole package, you may find yourself in the wrong place. In such situations, people may mishandle you because they don't understand your value and were never meant to be a part of your journey. It's important to recognise your worth and seek connections with those who appreciate and deserve you. Your value should not be diminished by mistreatment. Keep searching for the right environment and the right people who recognise and cherish your true value.

92

When you're at your lowest, you realise a lot.

When you're at your lowest ebb, you gain profound insights. In moments of struggle, you discover inner strength, resilience and clarity. Embrace these times as opportunities for growth and self-discovery. Pay attention to the lessons learned during your lows, as they can guide you towards a brighter future. Remember that even in the darkest moments, there is potential for transformation and positive change. Your lowest points can lead to some of your most profound realisations.

Silence is more powerful than proving your point.

In moments of conflict or disagreement, staying calm and composed can convey strength and wisdom. It allows you to listen, reflect and choose your battles wisely. Not every argument needs your response. Practise the art of silence to maintain your dignity and let the truth speak for itself. Sometimes, silence speaks louder than words and can resolve situations more effectively.

94

Sometimes the thing you want most is the thing you're best off without.

Recognise that what you desire most might not be what's best for you. Sometimes, our wants can lead us astray. Reflect on whether your deepest desires align with your true well-being and happiness. It's crucial to differentiate between what we think we need and what genuinely benefits us. Learning to let go of such desires can lead to a more fulfilling and balanced life. This self-awareness fosters personal growth and lasting contentment. What is one thing you can let go of?

They don't leave you for someone better, and they don't leave you for someone who's better looking.

They leave you for someone who's easier.

People may leave for various reasons, and it's not always about finding someone 'better' or 'more attractive'. Sometimes, it's about choosing an easier path. Don't take it as a reflection of your worth. Focus on your own growth and happiness. It's essential to be with someone who appreciates your value and is willing to put in the effort for a meaningful relationship. Understand that those who choose an easier route may not be the best fit for you. Your worth goes beyond convenience: seek relationships built on genuine connection and effort.

You're getting too comfortable again. Just remember what happened last time.

A gentle reminder: don't get too
comfortable in your current situation.
Recall the past when you stayed in your comfort zone.
Growth and progress often require stepping outside of
it. Embrace change and challenges to avoid stagnation.
Remember that your greatest achievements come when
you push beyond your comfort. Keep pushing your
boundaries, as it's where personal growth and new
opportunities await. Don't let fear of the unknown
hold you back; it's a path to a more fulfilling life.

97

Who is the person who saved you when you were at your lowest?

Think about the person who lifted you up when you were at your lowest point. They may have been a friend, a family member, or even yourself. Reflect on their support and love, and remember that you have the strength to overcome challenges. Gratitude for those who saved you can inspire resilience and remind you that you're not alone in difficult times. Surround yourself with a supportive network and continue to be your own saviour in moments of need. You have the power to rise above adversity with the help of those who care about you.

98

Part of healing is accepting that you'll never fully understand it.

Healing involves accepting that you may never fully understand the past or the pain. It's okay not to have all the answers. Focus on the present and your journey towards healing. Let go of the need to fully comprehend everything, as some things may remain a mystery. Embrace the process of healing, growth and self-discovery, and remember that healing doesn't always require complete understanding; it requires self-compassion, patience and resilience.

Focus on improving yourself, not proving yourself.

Direct your energy towards self-improvement, not the need to prove yourself to others. When you focus on yourself, you elevate your skills, knowledge and well-being. This inner progress speaks for itself and naturally gains respect from those who matter. Don't seek validation through others' opinions; instead, strive to be the best version of yourself. Your journey of improvement is a lifelong path that leads to self-fulfilment and success.

If it makes you happy, it doesn't have to make sense to anyone else.

Do what brings you joy, even if others don't understand it. Your happiness is personal and unique to you. Trust your instincts about what makes you feel fulfilled and content. Don't let the opinions or judgements of others sway you from your path to happiness. Remember, you're not obligated to explain or justify your sources of joy to anyone. Embrace what you love wholeheartedly, as long as it's healthy and positive for you.

Stop lying to yourself, and you'll unearth the profound truths that will set you free.

Sometimes, we deceive ourselves by downplaying situations or dismissing uncomfortable feelings. We convince ourselves it's not a big deal or that things will magically improve, but, deep down, do you truly believe that? Being brutally honest with yourself is like finding the key to unlocking your true potential. It's about embracing your authentic self – your strengths, weaknesses and all. When you stop the pretence and start being real, you'll uncover inner peace and genuine happiness, allowing you to become the best version of yourself. So remember, don't deceive yourself. Embrace who you are and you'll open the door to a more authentic and fulfilling life.

ACKNOWLEDGEMENTS

Many amazing individuals have played a part in bringing this book, *Stop Lying to Yourself*, to life. None more than my wife, Terri. Thank you for listening and guiding me at all stages throughout this amazing project. You have been my rock, my sounding board and my greatest supporter. Your contributions have been invaluable. From sending me ideas and helping me with wording to being a fantastic mum and stepmum, you have played a crucial role in shaping this book. You're my best friend, fan, critic and everything in between. Your strength, wisdom and unwavering belief in me have carried me through the toughest of times. Thank you for believing in me relentlessly, even when I didn't always believe in myself.

Thank you to my wonderful children, Reis, Kai, Danni, Frank and Dexter, for your unwavering support and love. You each remain my greatest achievements and fill me with more pride than any job ever could. Your presence in my life is a constant source of joy and inspiration. I am grateful for the love and encouragement you give me as I pursue my passions, and I hope to inspire you to reach for your dreams as well.

I want to express my heartfelt gratitude to my in-laws, Barbara and Garry, for their unwavering support and encouragement. Your belief in me has been a guiding light, and your presence in my life has been a source of strength and inspiration. Thank you for standing by me through thick and thin.

Thank you to my editor, Ru Merritt, for your support, patience and kindness in helping me turn this text into a book I could be proud of. Thank you to Abby Watson, Alice Brett, Morgana Chess, Catherine Ngwong and Jessica Anderson for all the work behind the scenes at Penguin.

Thank you to Giuseppe Zuccarello, Javier Guerra, Babu Chandarana and Andy Mardell for cheerleading me from the very beginning and listening without judgement when I needed advice or direction.

Thank you to all my amazing friends, I am so blessed to have you all in my life. And thank you to every single person who hit follow, like and share on any of my social media accounts. We have built such a kind, supportive and inspired community. I hope this book helps you all feel less alone and able to face life armed with some valuable tools you may need.

I love you all, take care,

Simon Gilham

@xgilham

ABOUT THE AUTHOR

Simon Gilham is an internationally successful CEO with a career spanning over 25 years. During the pandemic in 2020 he discovered an acute personal drive to self-improve and create a balanced mindset and life that were focused on perspective. Realising that his commitment and honesty in making hard decisions related to these goals were his strength, he went on to create a community sharing advice and prompts for others, through @xgilham.

This community has now grown to over 9 million people worldwide and acts as a reminder for us all that together it is easier to find the strength to navigate life's lows and amplify its highs. Simon lives in Kent with his wife and children and can be found on Instagram and TikTok at @xgilham. If you'd like to get in touch, please visit his website at www.xgilham.com.

@xgilham

@xgilham

@xgilham